I Am Smart

Written by Christine Taylor-Butler

Illustrated by Hector Borlasca

children's press ®

A Division of Scholastic Inc.

New York Toronto London Auckland Sydney
Mexico City New Delhi Hong Kong
Danbury, Connecticut

Library of Congress Cataloging-in-Publication Data

Taylor-Butler, Christine.
  I am smart / by Christine Taylor-Butler ; illustrated by Hector Borlasca.
     p. cm. — (My first reader)
  Summary: Although he is skinny and bookish and acts differently than other children, a young boy focuses on all the good things that make him special.
  ISBN 0-516-25176-7 (lib. bdg.)   0-516-24971-1 (pbk.)
  [1. Self-confidence—Fiction.] I. Borlasca, Hector, ill. II. Title. III. Series.
  PZ7.T2189Iam 2005
  [E]—dc22
                         2005004025

Note to Parents and Teachers

Once a reader can recognize and identify the 49 words
used to tell this story, he or she will be able to successfully
read the entire book. These 49 words are repeated throughout
the story, so that young readers will be able to recognize
the words easily and understand their meaning.

The 49 words used in this book are:

a	clothes	in	plain	this
am	do	is	read	too
and	don't	kids	say	use
are	ears	large	smart	volcano
at	fine	legs	some	way
big	fit	my	that	what
brain	hair	neat	the	work
build	help	not	there	write
can	I	other	thin	zoo
care	I'm	people	things	

Some kids say I don't fit in.

My ears are large.

My legs are thin.

My hair is neat.

My clothes are plain.

I do not care.

16

I use my brain.

There are things that I can do!

I help other people.

I work at the zoo!

I build a big volcano.

25

I read and write, too.

I don't care what some kids say.

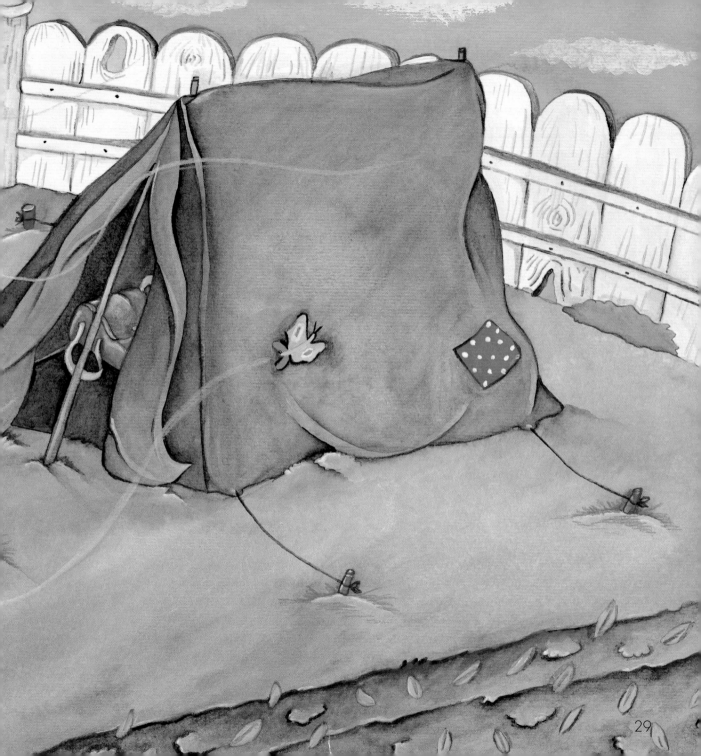

I am smart.

I'm fine this way!

ABOUT THE AUTHOR

Christine Taylor-Butler studied both Engineering and Art & Design at the Massachusetts Institute of Technology. When she's not writing stories for children, you'll find her buried in her mountain of books. She lives in Kansas City, Missouri, with her husband, two daughters, and many black cats.

ABOUT THE ILLUSTRATOR

Hector Borlasca was born in Buenos Aires, Argentina, where he currently resides with his wife Silvana and daughter, Micaela. He published his first illustration in Argentina at age 19. His work has appeared in advertising campaigns, magazines, newspapers, and textbooks. While not illustrating, Hector enjoys playing soccer and perfecting his tango.